MW00487954

Published by: Stone Inc.

Text Design by: Tanya Stone

Cover Design by: Tanya Stone

ISBN-13: 978-1-7333344-0-2
Distributed by:

Stone Inc.
Printed and bound in Location by KDP Publishing

For my Bird and Bee, my goddesses and every reason
why.

One day you'll find
all these scraps of me.
cobble them together
will you?
please don't say it's madness
call it art instead.

/call me crazy/

Call Me Crazy

TANYA STONE

Words are everything to her
more than stitched syllables
they are flights, caresses, and claws
she memorizes each one
suffers every lyric, the lover's ache
and spills her blood for ink on paper
carves offerings to your alter
and imagery for oration
but her true weight
that cuts the tongue
screams louder than hope
and renders the gypsy soul helpless
the most lethal of poisons
the waving of the white flag
when she surrenders her gifts
darkens the light from this world
silence.

/white flag/

You'll always be my almost
I'll never be your someday.

/almost always/

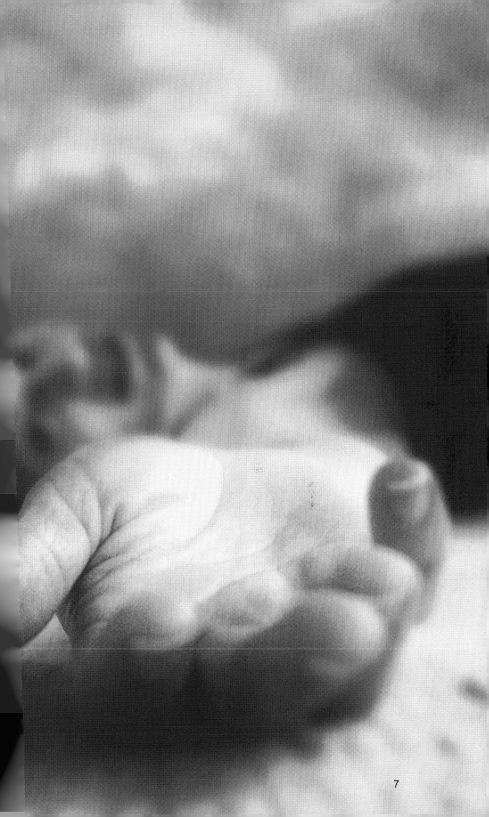

7

Her unkempt hair and chipped nails
are a warning to the traditional
and an invitation to the untamed
she's feral and undomesticated
choosing unpaved paths
seeking only a home with
walls of tangled legs and arms
an endless starlit roof
upon a foundation of wildflowers.

/feral/

She is boundless ecstasy
and bottomless sorrow
here I've made my home
insanely content
to neither sink nor float
finding another way
just to scream her name.

/between/

I chase butterflies
the ones in my garden
floating indiscriminate
any flower will do
I wish they'd land on me
and flutter against bare skin
like new love in clean sheets
the way my stomach feels
as your eyes land on me.

/butterflies/

I still jump
whether it was meant to be
or scrape my knees
no thought before the leap
I wish I could give you
this one gift
the gift of flight
even when you're unsure
of your wings.

/leap of faith/

14

Don't play it cool with me
I'm the lit match and poured kerosene
who prays for a strong wind to blow
so you better run
to me or from me
it doesn't matter
my heart is no place for the tepid
and I favor a fire to embers
let's burn up
bright
hot
fast
I am a wildfire
not meant to safely smolder
half dead and never alive a day.

/matchstick/

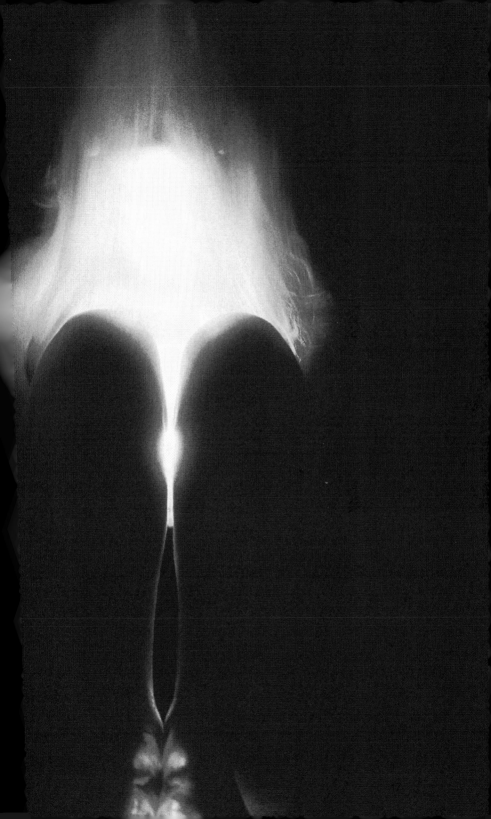

How long until morning
when someday is today
I'll run to you
I swear it
in all my finery
and sputter 'I Do'
out of turn
because I do you know
long for you
ache really
like that darkest moment
before dawn's promise.

/dawn's promise/

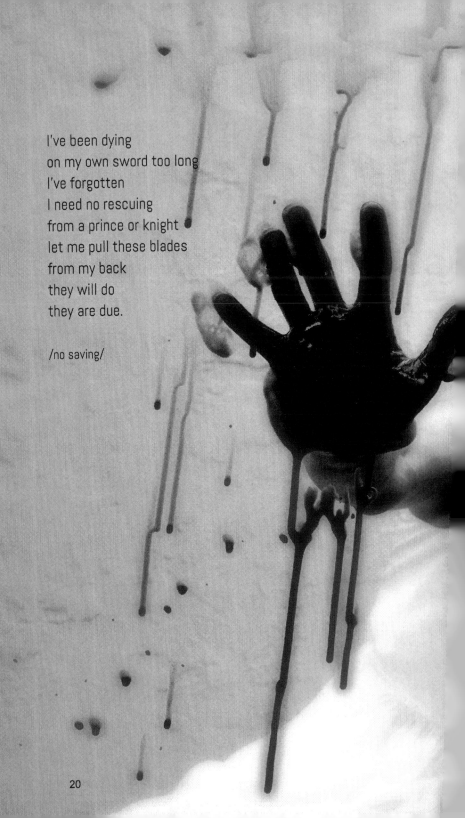

I've been dying
on my own sword too long
I've forgotten
I need no rescuing
from a prince or knight
let me pull these blades
from my back
they will do
they are due.

/no saving/

20

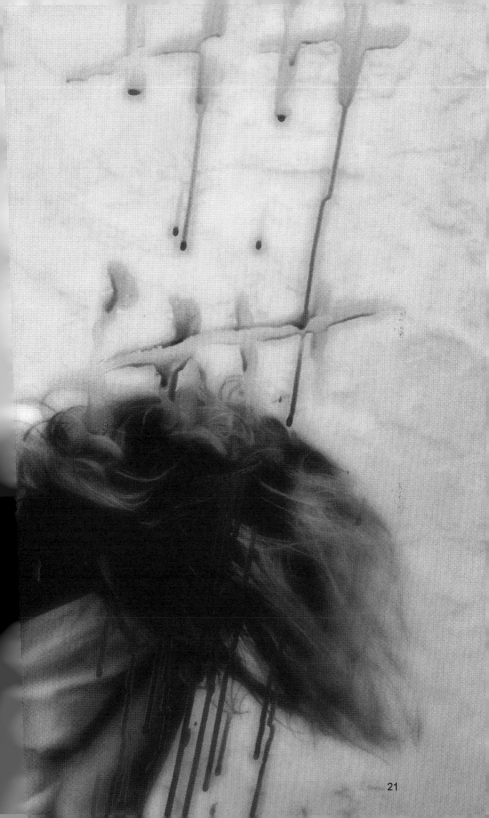

Oh to erase my words
as swiftly as you wipe away
the taste of my tongue.

/erase/

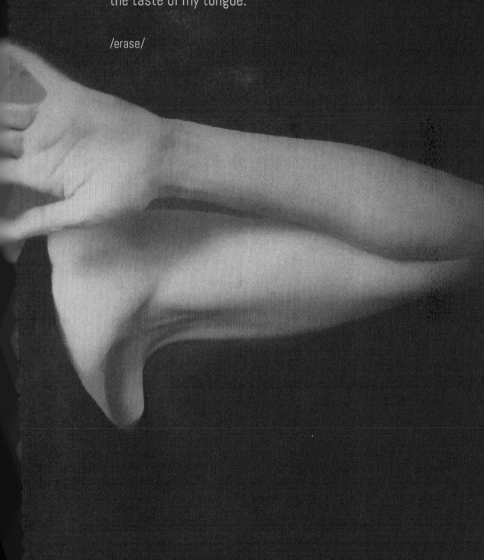

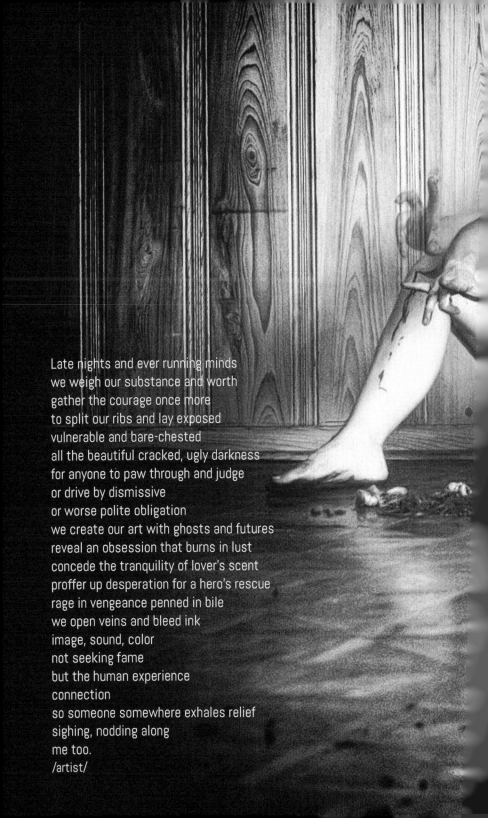

Late nights and ever running minds
we weigh our substance and worth
gather the courage once more
to split our ribs and lay exposed
vulnerable and bare-chested
all the beautiful cracked, ugly darkness
for anyone to paw through and judge
or drive by dismissive
or worse polite obligation
we create our art with ghosts and futures
reveal an obsession that burns in lust
concede the tranquility of lover's scent
proffer up desperation for a hero's rescue
rage in vengeance penned in bile
we open veins and bleed ink
image, sound, color
not seeking fame
but the human experience
connection
so someone somewhere exhales relief
sighing, nodding along
me too.
/artist/

25

She renamed the petals
until they whispered
I love Me
rather than She
and vowed to her garden
to plant more flowers
filled with promises
of self.

/gardener/

What an unfair exchange
your wishbone and funny bone
for a backbone
and stiff upper lip.

/exchange/

Beware the fair weather lust
basking in the warmth of sun
lust's wealth of blooming flowers
only burning on still nights
fretful coward in clouded sky
lust's desire dies at first frost
a late fall dawn over Boston
windows shut against the chill
but love
she is a subtle loyalty
constant harbor waves rolling
love walks in brave from storms
when your bones are broken
and cupboards are bare
love wraps your shameful skin
in worn blankets of grace
that smell of sea and home.

/love walks in/

I don't drown in my sorrows
I know how to swim
I will however
float with them if the light is just right
who can resist that golden hour
no matter the company.

/golden hour/

I'm no good at the waiting part
so instead I busy these hands
because everything's ending lately
and it's raining again
even when the sun is shining
while I'm looking for a rainbow
in these shades of grey.

/grey days/

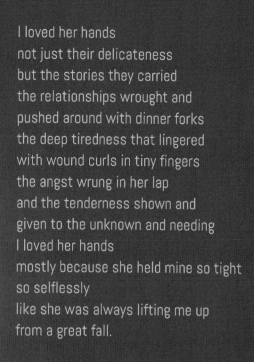

I loved her hands
not just their delicateness
but the stories they carried
the relationships wrought and
pushed around with dinner forks
the deep tiredness that lingered
with wound curls in tiny fingers
the angst wrung in her lap
and the tenderness shown and
given to the unknown and needing
I loved her hands
mostly because she held mine so tight
so selflessly
like she was always lifting me up
from a great fall.

/her hands/

To the perfect packaged women who don't extend invitations. Please stop. I'm human. I'm not your competition or judge because we are different. To my ex and the penance of our failed relationship. Please stop. I'm human. We cared about each other once. You don't have to break me to win. I tried my best to love you, to fit in. To the PTA mother who reminds me that I'm failing. Please stop. I'm human. I will miss fundraisers and my girl will be unprepared. I'm playing survival just like you. To the friends, peers, and loves that I fail to meet expectations. Please stop. I'm human. My body and spirit are in recovery. Grant me your graces now more than ever. Give me time and I will shine again. Maybe not. I'm perfectly human. And I'm going to forgive myself now. Hopefully someday you will too.

/human/

I'm driving too fast and chasing the moon
like we did so many nights ago
kissing in the middle of the road
I get to find something else to chase
even the heavens belong to you
it's too high already for me to catch
satiric like you
out of my reach
we are further apart now
than the space between stars
fated in constellations of beginnings
with no middle or end
bright sparks on a black sky canvas
each with the potential
to be as bright and hot as the sun
but too far and fast to ever really know
the sky is full of us tonight love
you are everywhere I look
and nowhere to be found
and my heart is undecided
whether I dread
or long for the night
when I look up
and only see the moon again.

/chasing you/

I pity the normal
their masked sanity
and wasted energy
to fool the masked
both sneaking glances
to judge and envy
the brazen artists
baring faces of truth
like Sunday's finest dress
while making mud pies
because it's Wednesday
and they can.

/wednesday/

I never did much mind
the suffering of love's slight
it was always the letting go
that undid me.

/grasp/

I get it
I understand our mothers now
your mom so angry and bitter
mine escaping to the imaginary life
yours with head in oven
locked away with her bottles
I feel their despair
that helplessness and anger
torn between the fairytale and what is
trapped and running in place
one day our daughters will feel us
they'll see we're from a place called Hell
and I became hard and you became kind
but that was never all we are
I'm not so tough and you're not weak
merely dressings to cover the holes
so the vultures would stop picking
circling our innards
no hiding the rot though
they come in the end for us
I look in the mirror
and all our mothers' eyes are mine
with trembling hands
I unravel the bandages.

/picking scabs/

In order to really reach me
you'll have to go deeper
than you've ever been before
beyond my hidden scars
and your own stories
past candied lips and honeyed words
further than my bared green heart
straight into my soul
and lay there with me
be shaken in panic
that you've never been so deep
inside another person ever
you may forget
lose your way
lose your mind
you may want to
stay.

/stay/

Hell's halls ring empty
as the devils dance untamed
you catch my eye wander
to my dance shoes by the door
disappointment sits between us
me for the dance
you for my longing.

/the dance/

Her back is
broader than
the grandest tales
burdens
jubilations
love made
wars waged
it cannot be confined
in the spine
of just one
book.

/her story/

She only knew
how to live
out loud
heart on her sleeve
blood on her knees
worried fingers
splintered lips
arms flung open
head thrown back
eyes to the sky
mouth grinning wide
mocking the moon
tears streaming down
sunken cheeks
spinning
spinning
spinning.

/truth serum/

I came to you for conquest
to devour or be consumed
for the rush of the ride
and what I found was solace
powerful, lifting, embracing
weightlessness and release
and I can't unfeel you now
I've found my true love.

/surf/

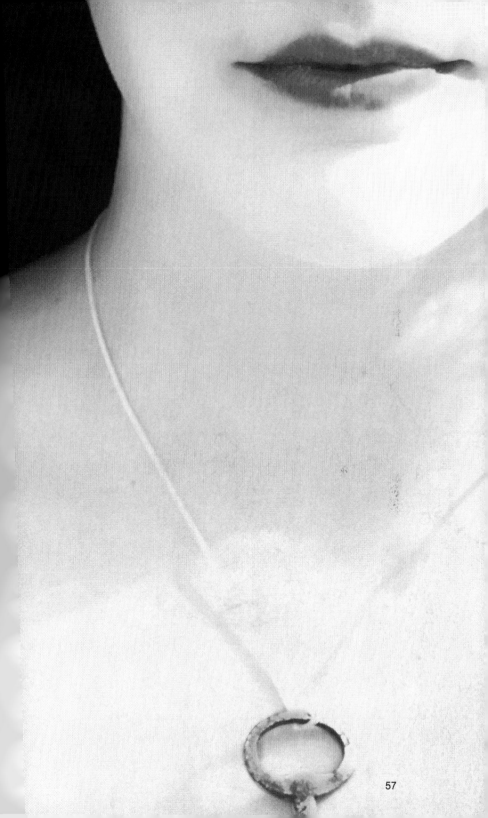

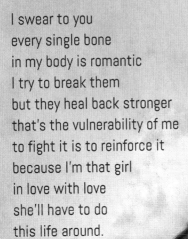

I swear to you
every single bone
in my body is romantic
I try to break them
but they heal back stronger
that's the vulnerability of me
to fight it is to reinforce it
because I'm that girl
in love with love
she'll have to do
this life around.

/hopeful romantic/

I miss you
the old you
I mourn the memories
hand drawn in charcoal
each feature etched
from memory
so many years ago
perfectly preserved in my heart
and when you returned to my arms
I swore I saw glimpses of you
when the mask fell from dead eyes
I loved you in those moments
every prayer answered
then abandoned
with dark desires
God, I miss you
the old you
the new you sucks.

/closet/

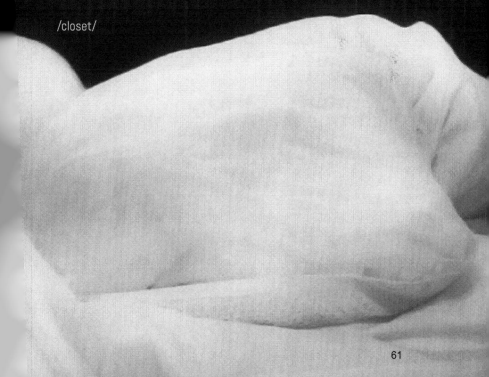

Let failure burn you
the hottest flames
that forge the strongest steel
and the sharpest swords
clears barren fields
to bear fruit again
only greatness
passes through flames
melting away impurity
and emerging the phoenix
shrugging ashes
from reborn wings.

/phoenix/

The space between
giving up and giving in
when I am on the brink
where I just might go mad
and it's ok with you
for me to not be ok
where I am controlled chaos
sleeping under the stars
at the drive-in theater
because I'm safe
in the grey pause
between settle and submit
there is peace
and now I understand
surrender.

/feminine/

Shake off my dress
save my soul.
wipe off my make up
save my life
no circus today
this clown is done
I surrender
sink

/bath/

Whoever added logic to love
hasn't been intimate a day in life
and the fool who adds pride
cannot comprehend
there is no space in desire's bed
because love sometimes looks like
arriving at your lover's door
three hours drive with no sleep
willing to say anything
not knowing if the door will open
because love has no use for reasoning
love won't let go because you tell it to
it waits
it fights
it burns
holds nothing back
so give me irrational passion
and all love's authentic lunacy
let me go mad in it's dance
all else is just sound without body.

/mirror/

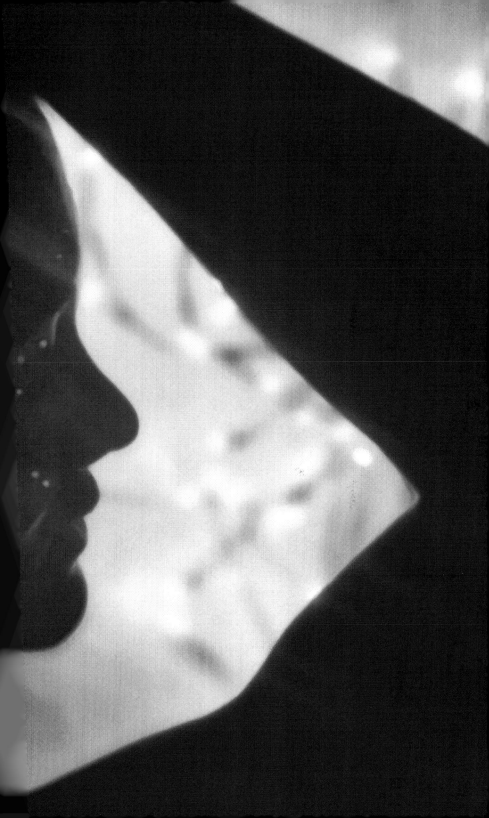

You're toxic
but I still lick the edges
craving the sting of you
on my tongue.

/battery/

Whatever happened to the good fight
and better make up sex
watered down now
with text messages
and digital emotions
I ache for the time
without screens and disconnect
when being in love
was a hands-on sport.

/make-up sex/

I will keep you
at an arms distance
and ever question
who could so love
this broken bird
while I hold my breath
praying you say "I do."

/unlovable child/

Don't tell me or yourself
you didn't know who I was
the girl afraid of loving
of never being enough
pushing and pulling
the one you never gave chase
I'm the same flower
fifteen years ago
twelve years from today
that you're too proud to pick
so go fill your nights
pretend we never danced
and on that day you forgive
and you're wondering
what country I'm in
when you hear bagpipes
and search crowds
for my face
come home.

/bagpipes/

The bravest thing
we can ever do
is to show someone
who we really are
and the bravest thing
they can do in return
is to love us and stay.

/authenticity/

No matter
if you passionately love a tiger
or venomously hate the beast
you'll never change its stripes
I would be a hypocrite to tell you
I hadn't believed I could
every
single
time.

/tiger's stripes/

I always bet the dark horse
not on the odds of first place
rather because if someone
anyone
just believes
maybe.

/trifecta/

This is the last stop
and I'm on the wrong side
of the right tracks
perfecting the art
of falling apart.

/track record/

Words are my weapons of choice
every time I cut you
I take a vow of silence
then reapply my lipstick.

/lipstick/

To be honest, the eggshell exterior was cracking for a while.
Maybe for months, years even.
I've lost track of time, pulling on my chains, treading water.
Spinning plates. Being everything outside and nothing inside.
Plotting my escape from the neo-hippy circus.
What was that dear? Yeah, go ahead and post that.
Look at us; perfectly crazy, fighting a fake world of materialism.
Perfectly.
Fighting.
Crazy.
Fake.
He's taking selfies with baby girl while I climb walls sinking
deeper in the pool of chameleon. Paddling further away from
course photocopies. He says to hurry and heal so we can do more,
go more places, plan more things.
More.
More.
More.
Not noticing I can barely breathe.
Is my head above water?
I can't tell and don't care which way is up.
What do I do?
No, what was it I wanted to be?
I'm sorry. So selfish.
What can I do for you?
What I have to do.
Or do nothing.
Surrender.
Float.
Release.
Sink.
Fill my lungs.

/neo-hippy circus/

When the devil knocks
answer the door
and put on your dancing shoes
you know you're gonna get burned
time and time again
but oh it is the devil
so dance, baby, dance
worry those wounds tomorrow
and tell yourself
even the devil
was made from angels once.

/when the devil knocks/

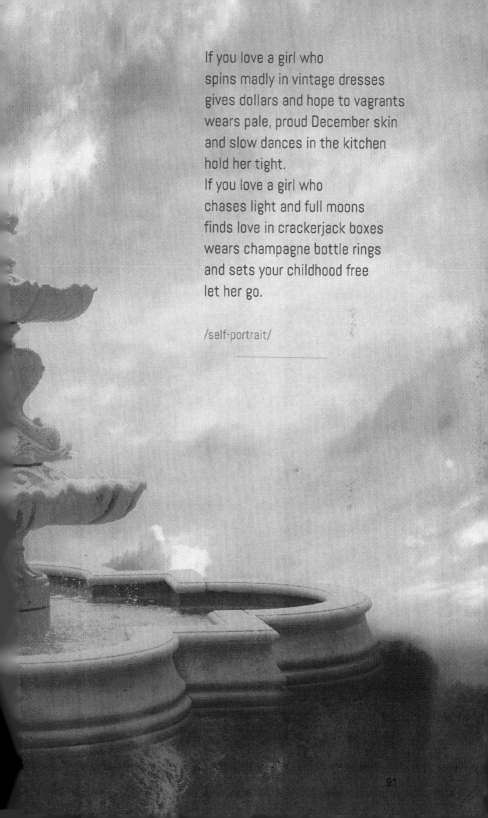

If you love a girl who
spins madly in vintage dresses
gives dollars and hope to vagrants
wears pale, proud December skin
and slow dances in the kitchen
hold her tight.
If you love a girl who
chases light and full moons
finds love in crackerjack boxes
wears champagne bottle rings
and sets your childhood free
let her go.

/self-portrait/

I seem like a good idea
but I'm every bit impossible
I'm a fighter
I like a good brawl
and great makeup sex after
a one-drink-too-many girl
who will rub your feet in apology
but I expect you there in the morning
if you're not
you're not for me
so go now
when the leaving is easy
or stay until time ends
there's no in-between.

/black and white/

she's pop rocks and vodka
candy and uncertain danger
double dare on your tongue
crazy sweet and unforgettable.

/candy/

And when the sun sets
I hope she is remembered
for all the little kindnesses
for the madness in her
kaleidoscope eyes
her head thrown back
arms open to the universe
and the art she bled
in words and image
for her soulmate
to have a beacon
this life and next.

/sunset/

She drank like a potion.
She burned like a curse.

/take your medicine/

I believe in karma
you better hope I'm wrong.

/karma/

Loosening the ties won't work
stop spinning the tales that bind you
change the story
drop the whole plot
I don't care how much time you invested and tangled you are
dig, damn it
cut yourself if you have to, but break free
rewrite yourself as ~~enough~~ GLORIOUS
be voluminous
take up space
make beautiful noise
because you are everything that matters
never shrink again
so others find you safe and worthy
because you are beyond comparison
and your genius is grander
than the tiny almosts
and not enoughs of this lifetime.

/the ties that bind/

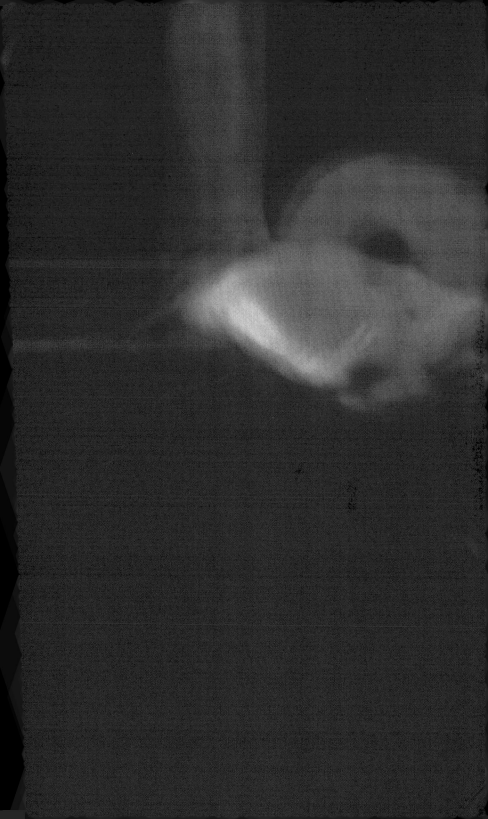

I saw you
looking over your shoulder
for a second glimpse at me
we have a story to tell
unfinished business
because I caught you
your second look
as I turned
for one more glance.

/unfinished business/

Don't call for rescue
she only revives me
to break my heart again.

/revival/

I would have married you on the Cliffs of Moher
instead of that gusty flight I whispered
in your ear that night on the floor
when I thought time would steal me
and you were all mine
I dreamed I could fold myself up inside you
make myself disappear
under those hands
and live in the crook of your arm
where the world ends and I begin
but you're searching for a different high
and I'm at an all time low
both on our knees
praying to feel
anything but life.

/cliffs of moher/

Every moment is so fleeting
like trying to savor sunshine
and there's a bittersweet sadness
to my head back, open-mouthed
trying to catch all of you
like snowflakes on my tongue
I think that's the genius of this life
time is water in clenched fists
slipping through desperate clinging
and I would be a fool to let go.

/ time/

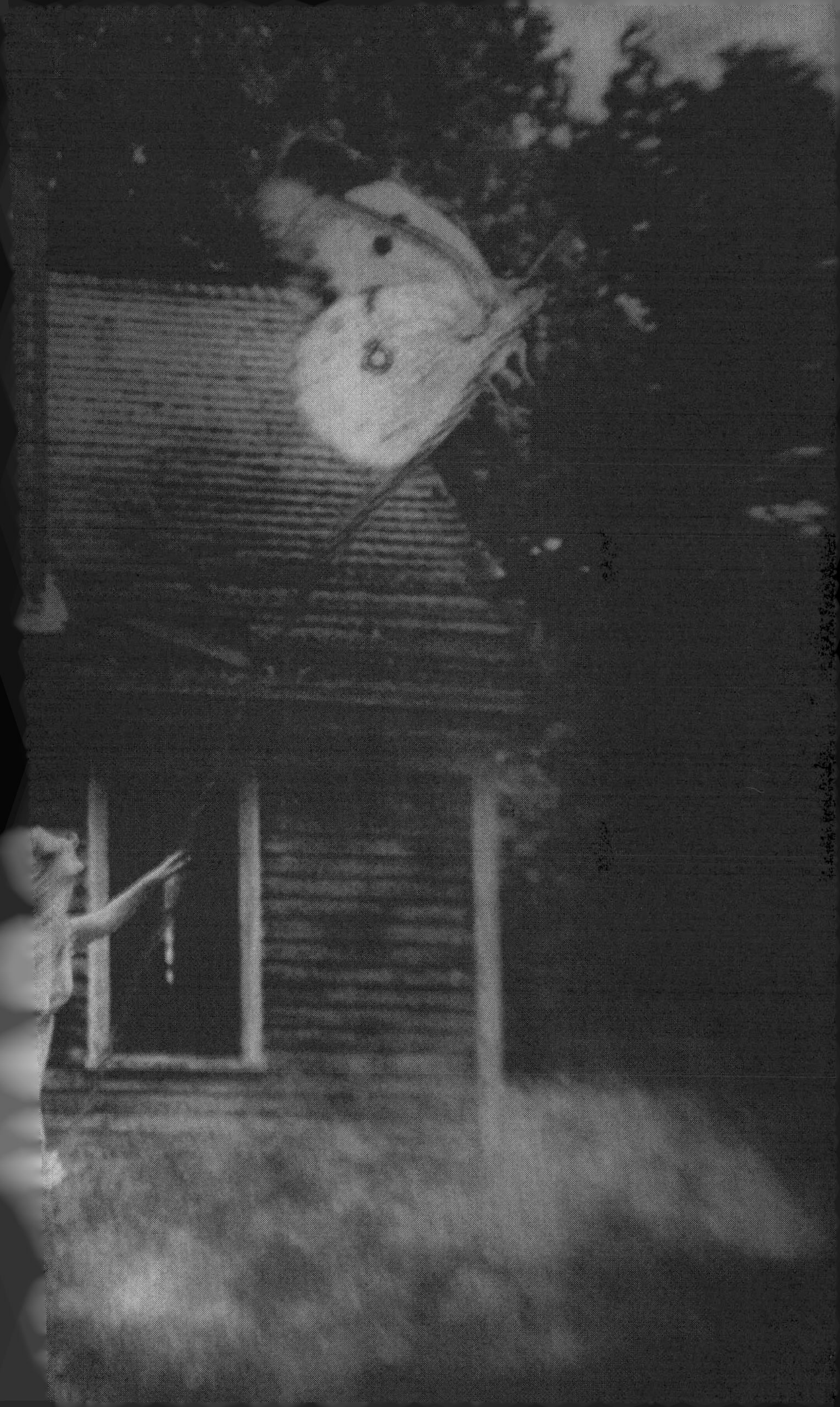

Forthcoming books from the talented Tanya Stone:

Eve - Poems All About Her and Fine Art Photography,
Stone, Inc. 2019

*The Dress Affairs - Short Stories and Photographic
Adventures,*
Stone, Inc 2020

Follow Tanya Stone on Instagram at #thetanyastone and
Facebook at Tanyastonestudios

Tanya Stone (born April 24, 1975) is an author, photographer, artist, and poet. She holds BA/BS degrees from University of Massachusetts, as well as an MBA from Florida Atlantic University for Business and Marketing. Although expressing an affinity for art and writing since childhood, she worked multiple corporate careers to include a 17-year career in Information Technology.
She formed her first corporation in her early thirties, and later formed Stone, Inc., which includes a clothing brand, and Tanya Stone Studios for her photography. She is self-taught in fine art self-portrait photography and digital composite art, and refers to herself as a "storyteller" who uses multiple means of expressions as a medium. She enjoys her well-rounded life as an avid traveller, business owner, and creator of clothing brand, Extra Dressing.

Tanya was born in New England and later moved to South Florida, where she resides today with her daughter.

58907088R00064

Made in the USA
Middletown, DE
08 August 2019